God's Will
for Your
Healing

GLORIA COPELAND

KENNETH
COPELAND
PUBLICATIONS

Unless otherwise noted, all scripture is from the *King James Version* of the Bible.

Scripture quotations marked *The Amplified Bible* are from *The Amplified Bible, Old Testament* © 1965, 1987 by the Zondervan Corporation. *The Amplified New Testament* © 1958, 1987 by The Lockman Foundation. Used by permission.

Scripture quotations marked *Weymouth* are from *The New Testament in Modern Speech* by Richard Francis Weymouth © 1996 Kenneth Copeland Publications.

God's Will for Your Healing
Reprinted from *God's Will for You* by Gloria Copeland

ISBN-10 0-93845-809-4   30-0503
ISBN-13 978-1-57562-253-8

18 17 16 15 14 13   23 22 21 20 19 18

© 1972 Gloria Copeland

Kenneth Copeland Publications
Fort Worth, TX 76192-0001

For more information about Kenneth Copeland Ministries, visit kcm.org or call 1-800-600-7395 (U.S. only) or +1-817-852-6000.

Table of Contents

Introduction

You must know it is God's will to heal you. Until this fact is settled in your mind and spirit, you cannot approach healing without being double minded and wavering. The Scripture says the double-minded man will receive nothing from the Lord (James 1:6-8).

You must know it is God's will to heal you.

The Word of God must abide in you concerning your healing. You have a covenant with God that includes divine health—every Christian does. The problem has been that most Christians do not know healing belongs to them.

The Holy Spirit, by the prophet Hosea, says, "My people are destroyed for lack of knowledge..." (Hosea 4:6). In the realm of healing, this scripture has been literally fulfilled. Christians have allowed sickness and disease to destroy their bodies. But God's Word says by His stripes we were healed (1 Peter 2:24). Believers are being physically destroyed because they are ignorant of the Word concerning their healing.

I The Word Is the Seed

In the parable of the sower, Jesus teaches that *the Word of God is the seed* and the hearts of men are the ground (Mark 4:14-20). The faith seed of the Word concerning your healing must be planted in your heart before you can successfully reap the healing harvest.

The Word says, "Being born again, not of corruptible seed, but of incorruptible, by the word of God, which liveth and abideth for ever" (1 Peter 1:23). The Word of God is the *incorruptible* seed. It cannot be spoiled or weakened by disease or any other force Satan has to offer. It has eternal life and power.

This incorruptible seed worked its power when you were born again. God's Word concerning salvation was planted in your heart and produced the faith to be saved.

Faith comes for healing the same way it came for salvation—by hearing the Word concerning healing. "So then faith cometh by hearing, and hearing by the word of God" (Romans 10:17).

There is no substitute for the seed—not even prayer. Faith comes only by hearing the Word. Praying for faith is a waste of time because God has already dealt to every born-again man *the measure* of faith (Romans 12:3). You received the faith of God when you were born again.

By hearing the Word, you continue to develop the faith for your healing. The force of that faith then rises up in you to receive God's healing power in your body.

> *By hearing the Word, you continue to develop the faith for your healing.*

Most Christians have no trouble believing they are saved and going to heaven. Most of the sermons they hear preached are about salvation, so that seed has been well planted, cultivated and watered. And when asked, "Is your name written in the Lamb's Book of Life?" most will say, without hesitation or doubt, "Yes, it is!" Have they seen the book? No—of course not. But they have confidence this is so because they have been taught that their name is written there. Even though they have not *seen* the book, they *believe*. That is faith in operation.

Faith concerning healing should be as highly developed in the Church as is faith concerning salvation. If the Church were told what the Word says about healing, Christians would be equally as quick to believe they are healed as to believe they are saved. However, instead of teaching and preaching that healing belongs to us, many have taught just the opposite.

It is easy to understand why the Church as a whole has not walked in divine health for all these years, even though healing has belonged to it. Men have tried to teach God's Word through head knowledge, instead of *by His Spirit,* which sowed traditions and seeds of doubt. Jesus said that men make the commandment of God of no effect by their tradition (Matthew 15:6).

One tradition tells us healing was just to get the early church started and has passed away. Another tradition says God heals *some* people, but you never know if He will heal *you.*

Tradition and the Thorn in the Flesh

Tradition teaches that Paul's thorn in the flesh was sickness or disease. The Word plainly tells us this thorn was a messenger from Satan—a personality. (The word for *messenger* is also translated in other New Testament verses as "angel.")

Watch this messenger of Satan deal Paul blow after blow in the following scriptures: "But when the Jews saw the multitudes, they were filled with envy, and spake against those things which were spoken by Paul, contradicting and blaspheming. But the Jews stirred up the devout and honourable women, and the chief men of the city, and raised persecution against Paul and Barnabas, and expelled them out of their coasts" (Acts 13:45, 50).

After the incident at Antioch, the apostles shook the dust from their feet and went to Iconium. They spoke boldly in the Lord, and the Lord proved the Word by granting signs and wonders done by their hands.

And when there was an assault made both of the Gentiles,
and also of the Jews with their rulers, to use them despite-
fully, and to stone them, they were ware of it, and fled unto
Lystra.... And there came thither certain Jews from Antioch
and Iconium, who persuaded the people, and, having
stoned Paul, drew him out of the city, supposing he had
been dead. Howbeit, as the disciples stood round about
him, he rose up, and came into the city: and the next day
he departed with Barnabas to Derbe (Acts 14:5-6, 19-20).

The men from Antioch and Iconium who were filled with
envy brought the persecution against Paul in Lystra. But they
were only *instruments* used by the *source* of persecution—the
messenger of Satan. Wherever Paul went, the evil spirit
worked to incite the people against him. *He* was the thorn in
Paul's side.

The Lord told Moses that if the Israelites did not drive out
the inhabitants of the land of Canaan, those inhabitants would
vex them and be pricks in their eyes and thorns in their sides
(Numbers 33:55).

In like manner, Paul describes this evil angel as a thorn in
his side: "...There was given me a thorn in the flesh, Satan's
angel to torture me" (2 Corinthians 12:7, *Weymouth*). Paul
had received an abundance of revelation, and Satan came to
snatch that Word away (Mark 4:15).

The Word that is alive in you is the Word you steadfastly

act on. However, you will have to stand in faith for every word of revelation knowledge you receive, just as Paul did. Satan will see to it that no believer is exalted above the measure of the Word that actually *lives* in him. God had given Paul the revelation of the authority of the believer. He had authority over Satan in the Name of Jesus, just as you do. To get results, Paul had to *enforce* this authority by directly commanding the evil spirit to desist in his maneuvers against him.

"For this thing I besought the Lord thrice, that it might depart from me" (2 Corinthians 12:8). If you want results, do not ask God to deal with the devil for you. Just as God told Moses to drive out the inhabitants of the land, He instructs *you* to drive out the demons or evil spirits yourself (Mark 16:17). "Submit yourselves therefore to God. Resist the devil, and he will flee from you" (James 4:7).

God has given you the Name of Jesus and the authority to use that Name in binding Satan and his forces. God will not deal with Satan for you; but when you take the Name of Jesus and the Word of God and command him to stop his attack against you, all of heaven *guarantees* results.

Paul himself writes by the Spirit in Ephesians 6:12, "For we wrestle not against flesh and blood, but

> *When you take the Name of Jesus and the Word of God and command Satan to stop his attack against you, all of heaven guarantees results.*

against principalities, against powers, against the rulers of the darkness of this world, against spiritual wickedness in high places." You speak directly to Satan and his evil spirits in the Name of Jesus and cast them out!

When Paul asked the Lord to make this messenger of Satan depart from him, the Lord said, "My grace is sufficient for thee: for my strength is made perfect in weakness..." (2 Corinthians 12:9). He did not say that the messenger would not depart. He was saying to Paul, "My favor is enough. For when you do not have the ability to humanly overcome, you use *My* name to stop Satan's attack, and *My* power will excel in your behalf. My favor is enough. *You* cast out the devil."

The Greek word *dunamis,* translated "strength" in 2 Corinthians 12:9, is the same word translated "power" when Jesus said, "Ye shall receive power, after that the Holy Ghost is come upon you..." (Acts 1:8). The more literal translation is "power." *Weymouth* reads, "My grace suffices for you, for power is perfected in weakness." (This is the opposite of tradition's teaching that Paul had no victory over the thorn in the flesh.)

Then Paul said, "Most gladly therefore will I rather glory in my infirmities, that the power of Christ may rest upon me. Therefore I take pleasure in infirmities, in reproaches, in necessities, in persecutions, in distresses for Christ's sake: for when I am weak, then am I strong" (2 Corinthians 12:9-10). The Greek word translated *infirmities,* means "want of strength, weakness, indicating inability to produce results."[1] Paul lists these buffetings—prisons, stoning, beatings, shipwrecks and angry mobs—in detail in 2 Corinthians 11:23-28. However, sickness is not mentioned.

When the mob came after Paul to stone him, he had no strength, or power, in himself to overcome the situation. Twice the Lord's grace proved sufficient, and he escaped out of their hands.

In Lystra, they actually stoned Paul. Thinking he was dead, they took him out of the city. But God had said, "My grace is sufficient for thee," and as the disciples stood around him, he rose and went on his way. Paul had no strength to stop that angry mob. When he was physically helpless, God's power was displayed mightily and wrought great deliverance for him. Paul was not strong in himself, but he was strong in the Lord and in the power of His might.

Satan's angel, the thorn in the flesh, could gain no victory over Paul through adverse circumstances because the power of Christ rested upon him. He said, "I have learned in any and all circumstances the secret of facing every situation..." (Philippians 4:12, *The Amplified Bible*). In the next verse, Paul shares this secret with you: "I have strength for all things in Christ Who empowers me [I am ready for anything and equal to anything through Him Who infuses inner strength into me]...."

When Paul in himself was weak, Paul in Christ was

strong. Of these afflictions and persecutions Paul wrote
Timothy: "Persecutions, sufferings—such as occurred to me at
Antioch, at Iconium, and at Lystra, persecutions I endured,
but out of them all the Lord delivered me" (2 Timothy 3:11,
The Amplified Bible).

The Lord delivered him out of them all! He lived to be an
old man and then said that he could not decide whether to
stay here or to go to be with the Lord. He needed to stay here
for the Church's sake but yearned to be with Jesus. Paul did
not leave this world until he and the Lord were ready. Satan's
angel, that thorn in the flesh we have heard so much about,
never did overcome Paul and the power of God. Satan could
do no more than vex him and be a thorn in the flesh. Paul
was a covenant man; he ran the race and won. Paul preached
the Word throughout the world, wrote most of the New
Testament and caused revival wherever he went. When
human strength ends, the power of God excels.

Paul's thorn in the flesh is another tradition that Satan has
used to deceive and rob the Church.

Tradition says God gets glory from sickness because
the world sees how marvelously the Christian bears the
pain and agony. (Tradition never produces the right answer.)
Anyone knows that the world has all the pain and agony it
can stand. What the world wants is a way *out* of sickness—
not a way *into* it. Suffering has no appeal to the world;
but through tradition, Satan has sold suffering to the

Church as being the will of God.

How helpless you are in the face of Satan and disease without the seed of the Word of God living in you concerning your healing! And if you allow the traditions of men to usurp authority over God's Word, you will continue to be helpless in the face of sickness. God will be able to do nothing for you—you will have made His Word "of none effect" in your life.

The Word of God is incorruptible seed. Satan does not have the power to stop it. Disease does not have the power to overcome it. In your life only *you* have the power to stop the Word from working.

> *The Word of God is incorruptible seed. Satan does not have the power to stop it.*

Lay aside what tradition has taught you. Your heart has never agreed with it anyway. Realize that only Satan could be the source of such powerless, defeated beliefs sold to the family of Almighty God.

As you study the Word of God concerning healing, this incorruptible seed of the Word will drive out the doubt and tradition you have been taught.

3 A Study of the Heart

"And the very God of peace sanctify you wholly; and I pray God your whole spirit and soul and body be preserved blameless unto the coming of our Lord Jesus Christ" (1 Thessalonians 5:23).

Man *is* a spirit. He has a soul made up of his reasoning faculties, will and emotions, and he lives in a physical body.

The heart of man is the spirit of man. Your spirit is the real you. (Do you *have* a human? No, you *are* a human. You do not *have* a spirit. You *are* a spirit.)

Man thinks of himself as being only a body because he cannot see his spirit with the natural eye. But to understand spiritual things, it is important that you realize *you are a spirit.*

This "new creature" or the "hidden man of the heart," as the Scripture calls him, is the spirit, the real man. This is the part of you that was re-created the righteousness of God when you were born again. Your mind and body were not made new but *you* (the man) were re-created. "Therefore if any man be in Christ, *he is a new creature:* old things are passed away; behold, all things are become new" (2 Corinthians 5:17).

"But let it be the hidden man of the heart, in that which is not corruptible, even the ornament of a meek and quiet spirit, which is in the sight of God of great price" (1 Peter 3:4). The real man is hidden to the natural eye. You can see only the man's body. Paul speaks of the body as "the clothing of the spirit" and the "tent which is our earthly home" (2 Corinthians 5:1-8, *The Amplified Bible).* Your body is a *covering* for your spirit.

In the same text, Paul speaks of being absent from the body and being present with the Lord. When the man, or the spirit, leaves the body, the body dies. The spirit is the life of the body. The spirit can live independently of the body, but the body cannot live without the spirit.

The spirit does not die. The spirit of man will live forever, with either his god Satan or with the Lord Jesus Christ. When a man dies, he does not cease to exist; he only ceases to live in the physical body.

The spirit is called the heart of a man because it is the core, or center, of his being. The heart of a tree is the core of that tree. The heart of a watermelon is called that because it is the center of the melon. (Not because it pumps watermelon juice!) Anytime the Scripture speaks of the heart, you know it is not speaking of the physical blood pump but the real man or the spirit.

First Plant the Seed

Many try to reap the healing harvest without first planting the seed. "Until the person seeking healing is sure from God's Word that it is God's will to heal *him,* he is trying to reap a harvest where there is no seed planted."[2]

Can you imagine a farmer at planting time sitting down on his front porch and saying, "I am going to believe for a crop this year. I believe in crops and know they are real, but I will not plant the seed. I will just believe."

Unless the farmer planted the seed, he would have no basis for faith. No matter how hard he tried to believe, he would have nothing in the ground to produce the harvest.

Unless the farmer planted the seed, he would have no basis for faith.

Even if you believe in healing, without the healing seed from God's Word planted in your heart, you have nothing in the ground to produce the harvest. You have no real basis for faith. Neither you nor the farmer will reap the harvest—unless you first plant the seed.

Believing in healing is not enough. You must *know* that it is God's will for *you* to be healed.

Allow the faith seed of the Word of God concerning your healing to be planted in you, and you can successfully reap the healing harvest.

Through the Word, you can know without a doubt it is God's unchanging will for you to be healed.

The Heart of Man Is the Ground

The Scripture tells us that God provided the seed for the sower (2 Corinthians 9:10). God has already given you the incorruptible seed—the Word of God.

He has not only provided you with the seed, but He has prepared the ground. The heart of man is the ground in which the seed of the Word is planted. When you were born again by His Holy Spirit, your heart was created in His image. "And that ye put on the new man, which after God is created in righteousness and true holiness" (Ephesians 4:24).

At one time your heart was corrupt. You had the nature of spiritual death and could produce only sin. Now you are a *new* man created in God's image.

"For he hath made him to be sin for us, who knew no sin; that we might be made the righteousness of God in him" (2 Corinthians 5:21). God paid a great price to make you good ground for His Word. Through the sacrifice of His Son Jesus, He has **made** you the righteousness of God.

> *God paid a great price to make you good ground for His Word.*

The good ground of your heart was created by His power

to be the dwelling place for His Spirit and His Word. Not only that, but the force of faith was born into this new creature.

If you have been born again, you have faith. You may not have known how to use it, but faith has been born into you. It is the same faith with which God created the world. It is by this force issuing out of the heart that the Word, the seed, brings forth fruit.

Jesus teaches us some very important things concerning the good ground of the heart and the seed of the Word.

Satan Steals the Word

"The sower soweth the word. And these are they by the way side, where the word is sown; but when they have heard, Satan cometh immediately, and taketh away the word that was sown in their hearts" (Mark 4:14-15).

The Word was sown and went into the heart. It is the incorruptible seed and would have produced after its kind, but believers allowed Satan to take the Word out of their hearts.

Satan snatches the Word away through doubt, unbelief and tradition. He does everything in his power to keep the Word from abiding in your heart in order to keep you unproductive. The seed was taken out of the ground; therefore, it could produce no harvest and Satan's work continued unhindered.

Stony Ground

"And these are they likewise which are sown on stony ground; who, when they have heard the word, immediately receive it with gladness; and have no root in themselves, and so endure but for a time: afterward, when affliction or persecution ariseth for the word's sake, immediately they are offended" (Mark 4:16-17).

The stony ground did not allow the seed to take root. These people believed the Word *until* trouble came. Then they had no confidence to *act* on the Word. The Word had no root.

When you receive revelation knowledge from the Word, Satan will test and try you to get the Word out of your heart.

> *The Word is no threat to Satan until it is put into the heart of man.*

There is no way seed can produce fruit unless it is in the ground. The Word is no threat to Satan until it is put into the heart of man.

Notice this verse said affliction came *because of the Word*. When you receive the Word on healing, Satan will attempt to make you sick so that you will be offended and let go of the Word that was put in your heart. He will *try* to make you sick, but he *cannot* if you will resist him. However, if you allow yourself to be stony ground, when trouble comes you will be offended and fall away from the

Word. You will let the Word wither away in your heart
before it can take root.

When feelings or circumstances looked contrary to
the Word that was sown, these people let the Word go
and believed what they could see.

Thorns in the Heart

"And these are they which are sown among thorns; such
as hear the word, and the cares of this world, and the deceitfulness of riches, and the lusts of other things entering in,
choke the word, and it becometh unfruitful" (Mark 4:18-19).

Be cautious of the thorns of life. The cares of this world,
the deceitfulness of riches and the lust of other things are dan-
gerous weapons of the enemy. They enter into the heart and
choke the Word until the Word cannot produce.

These people have given their thought, life and energy to
the cares of this world, running after riches and the lusts of
their flesh. They have set their minds on and pursued those
things that gratify the flesh. The Scripture teaches that the
mind of the flesh is death (Romans 8:5-6).

Thorns in the heart are deadly.

This is directly opposite of what God told Joshua to
do in order to make his way prosperous and have good
success. He told Joshua to meditate in His Word day and

night, to set his mind on the Word.

You, like Joshua, are admonished to set your affections on things that are above and not on things that are on the earth (Colossians 3:2). Oh, yes! It is to your great advantage because to be spiritually minded is life and peace (Romans 8:6). We have God's Word that when we seek first His kingdom, all these other things will be added unto us (Matthew 6:33).

The same formula God gave Joshua still works today. God has given the formula for success. He has given the seed. He has prepared the ground of your heart to receive that seed, but you must use the formula.

You set your affections. This is a matter of your will. *You* set your mind on those things that gratify your flesh (five senses), or *you* set your mind on those things that gratify the spirit. God *cannot* do that part for you.

It has not been the ground that has prevented the Word from bearing fruit in any of these illustrations but the things that were allowed *in* the ground—Satan, the stones and the thorns.

Give the Word first place in your life in order to be good ground for the Word!

Good Ground

"And these are they which are sown on good ground; such as hear the word, and receive it, and bring forth fruit, some thirtyfold, some sixty, and some an hundred" (Mark 4:20).

You have learned from the previous scriptures what will keep your heart from being good ground. Now Jesus teaches how to be good ground for the Word, and thereby produce the harvest.

The Word of God is the will of God. When the Word is planted in good ground—free from hindrances—the crop produced will be God's will for your life.

The law of Genesis is that everything brings forth fruit after its own kind. You plant the Word of God in your heart, water and cultivate that Word, and it will bring forth the fulfillment of that Word in your life.

Look at the hearts that were called stony ground. They heard the Word and received it with joy. That was not enough! When trouble came, they had no confidence in what they had heard. They were moved by what they saw, rather than by the Word of God. Circumstances scorched the seed, and it withered away before it could take root. Good ground hears the Word, understands it and acts on it.

Bringing forth fruit is acting on the Word. Acting on the Word germinates the seed—causes it to sprout and take root.

Faith is acting on God's Word regardless of what you see. Faith brings forth the crop.

The time that you must hold fast to God's Word is when trouble comes. It is the man who will hold fast to his confession of the Word in the hard places and the crises that will obtain faith's results.

Acting on the Word is the difference between stony ground and good ground.

The soil brings forth fruit *before* the crop is harvested. You are the good ground. You must act on the Word before you see the results. "For we walk by faith, not by sight" (2 Corinthians 5:7).

"Therefore I say unto you, What things soever ye desire, when ye pray, believe that ye receive them, and ye shall have them" (Mark 11:24). You believe that you receive *when you pray* and *before you see* because God's Word says the answer belongs to you. And, according to Jesus, you shall have what you desire from the Father.

Good ground *hears* the Word, *receives* the Word and *does* the Word.

Jesus tells us the thrilling result of the seed of the Word planted in good ground. "If ye abide in me, and my words abide in you, ye shall ask what ye will, and it shall be done unto you" (John 15:7).

I Am the Lord
That Healeth Thee

Healing was not introduced during the ministry of Jesus, nor is it only a New Covenant blessing. This comes as a surprise to many who are trying to believe that God wants to heal them. God has always provided healing for His people through His covenants.

He revealed Himself as the Great Physician when He told Israel that if they would obey His Word, none of the diseases of Egypt would come upon them. He said, "...For I am the Lord that healeth thee" (Exodus 15:26).

When God gave Israel the blessing of the law, He said if they would hearken *diligently* to the voice of the Lord and be careful to do His commandments, the blessings would come upon them and overtake them.

He placed Himself as Israel's healer, Jehovah-Rapha.

Healing was not an automatic blessing but was conditional, based on diligently obeying His Word.

"Fools because of their transgression, and because of their

iniquities, are afflicted. Then they cry unto the Lord in their trouble, and he saveth them out of their distresses. He sent his word, and healed them, and delivered them from their destructions" (Psalm 107:17, 19-20). Disease came through disobedience to the law. Forgiveness for that disobedience brought healing to their bodies.

God provided an umbrella of protection and blessing for His people through His Word. When they sinned, they broke the covenant, and they took themselves from under its protection.

> *God provided an umbrella of protection and blessing for His people through His Word.*

As long as Israel kept the covenant with God, no disease was powerful enough to come upon them. When they turned away from God's Word, disease filled their bodies.

When Israel got out from under God's protection by disobedience, the curse that was *already* upon the earth overtook them. The whole world was under the curse that came when Adam changed gods and Satan became his ruler.

All Israel had to do was to be like the other nations and the curse would come upon them. Without acting on God's Word, Israel became helpless in the face of poverty, sickness, fear and her enemies.

The Origin of Sickness

Our Father is the God of Love and from the beginning has desired for His people freedom from the curse that came upon the earth when Adam committed high treason.

Adam's sin of high treason was not God's will. Adam was a free man and ruler of the earth. God had given him this domain and Adam *by his own will* made Satan lord and father over him.

The nature of spiritual death replaced God's life in Adam's spirit. Sickness came into this world order on the wings of spiritual death. Man was not sick before he died spiritually.

Adam's sin was not God's will—neither are the *results* of that sin God's will. Satan, through the Fall of man, is the origin of the curse and all its effects.

Sin manifests in the spirit. Sickness manifests in the body. Both are the result of Satan and the rulership that man committed to him in the Fall. Both are works of evil. Neither is from the hand of God.

If God's will had been sickness and death, He would have placed them in the Garden Himself. He would not have wrought sickness or sin by the hand of His enemy.

It was necessary for Israel to diligently hearken to God's Word. The curse was a powerful force. It had overtaken the whole world. God was not being hard or demanding by

Only God's Word— a power greater than evil—could stop the effect of the curse.

putting a burden on His people through the statutes and ordinances. Only His Word—a power greater than evil—could stop the effect of the curse.

Keeping God's covenant was Israel's *only* deliverance.

God Is Not the Thief

We must understand that the laws governing the earth largely came into being with the Fall of man and the curse on the earth. Because of this, many accuse God of the accidents that take place, of the sickness and death of loved ones, of storms and catastrophes, of earthquakes and floods that continually occur.

All these natural laws came with the Fall. Satan is their author, and when Satan is finally eliminated from human contact, or rather, from the earth, these laws will stop functioning.[3]

After Satan is cast into the lake of fire, there will be no tears, no death, no sorrow and no pain on the earth. The source of these evil works will be bound and tormented day and night forever and ever. "And God shall wipe away all tears from their eyes; and there shall be no more death, neither sorrow, nor crying, neither shall there be any more pain: for the former things are passed away" (Revelation 21:4).

The origin of sickness and disease is as obvious as the origin of sin. Jesus said, "The thief cometh not, but for to steal, and to kill, and to destroy: I am come that they might have life, and that they might have it more abundantly" (John 10:10).

God is not the thief! Satan has come to steal from you, kill you and destroy you in any way that he can. Until you find out from the Word what belongs to you, he will continue to distress and manipulate your life.

Most people, even Christians, blame God for Satan's work because they do not realize that it is only through the intervention of the Body of Christ in the affairs of earth that God is able to bless humanity today. "We know [positively] that we are of God, and the whole world [around us] is under the power of the evil one" (1 John 5:19, *The Amplified Bible*).

All the authority and dominion the Church does not actively enforce is under the sway and power of Satan, not because it is God's will, but because man originally gave Satan dominion over him. Even though *Jesus has taken that dominion away* from Satan, the Church still has to enforce its authority in the earth.

Because of our enemy, this authority will not operate passively. It will not work automatically, but must be *enforced*. In ignorance of God's Word, the Church has allowed Satan to steal its authority and, for the most part, to control the earth.

Jesus conquered Satan in his own domain. "And having

spoiled principalities and powers, he made a show of them openly, triumphing over them in it" (Colossians 2:15).

The Amplified Bible says, "[God] disarmed the principalities and powers that were ranged against us and made a bold display and public example of them...."

"And the hostile princes and rulers He stripped off from Himself, and boldly displayed them as His conquests..." *(Weymouth)*. Weymouth says in a footnote that *princes and rulers* was literally translated "authorities and powers."

Jesus took by conquest all the authority that Adam had given Satan in the Fall. Jesus, the Son of God, stripped Himself, became like man and was born a human being so that, as a man, He could conquer Satan and take back from him all the authority that belonged to Adam.

Jesus incapacitated and paralyzed Satan. Satan has been disarmed—he has no weapons where the Church is concerned. All the earthly power and authority Satan has is now useless against the Church of Jesus Christ.

Jesus gave the power of attorney to the Church before He ascended and sat down at the right hand of the Father. He said, "All power is given unto me in heaven and in earth. Go ye therefore..." (Matthew 28:18-19). "And these signs shall follow them that believe; In my name shall they cast out devils; they shall speak with new tongues; they shall take up serpents; and if they drink any deadly thing, it shall not hurt them; they shall lay hands on the sick, and they shall recover" (Mark 16:17-18).

Jesus said, "*All* power—ability to do or act—has been given to Me. Therefore, you go in My name and these signs shall follow *you.*" He authorized the Church to use His Name with all its vast authority. The word *authorize* means "to give official approval or legal power; to give right to act; to empower."

In the Great Commission, Jesus proved that in His Name believers were not limited by the natural laws that had governed the earth since Satan began to rule.

"They shall cast out devils...." In the Name of Jesus—because that Name has all authority in heaven and in earth invested in it—the believer has the power to cast out devils. (Man did not have authority over Satan under the old covenant. Only under the protection of the law could he enjoy any kind of freedom from distress. He did not deal with Satan directly.)

"They shall speak with new tongues...." The natural limitations of speech were removed. Now the believer can talk in the spirit with the Lord. No longer limited by his lack of understanding, the new man in Christ, filled with His Spirit, can speak mysteries unto his God (1 Corinthians 14:2).

"They shall take up serpents; and if they drink any deadly thing, it shall not hurt them...." If a believer accidentally drinks poison or gets a snakebite, the Name of Jesus spoken in faith will stop the deadly effects, even though natural law says these are fatal. You see record of this in Paul's ministry when the deadly viper attached itself to his hand and the natives of Malta waited for him to die (Acts 28:1-6). Natural law had no power over him because he was operating under the jurisdiction of the Name of Jesus. Death did not have the power to overcome this authority!

"They shall lay hands on the sick, and they shall recover." Not all the sick in the world will recover, but those on whom the believer lays hands in the Name of Jesus will recover. The law of sickness and disease that has worked practically unhindered since the Fall of man must cease to operate at the command of a believer in the Name of Jesus!

Just as in the days of old, the curse is still a powerful force today, and only a power greater than evil can stop the effect of that curse.

The Name of Jesus is greater than the curse. The Name of Jesus is greater than the curse. The Word of God is greater than the curse. The Holy Spirit is greater than the curse.

These three weapons make the believer greater and more powerful than the curse of sin, sickness, fear and poverty.

Jesus said, "I will not leave you comfortless" (John 14:18). He kept His Word. He sent the Holy Spirit to teach you the truths and laws of the world of the spirit. These truths of the Spirit are more powerful and will supersede the natural laws that govern the earth. They do not nullify natural laws; but just as the law of gravity can be superseded by the law of lift, God's laws of the spirit are higher than the laws of the physical world.

God, by His Spirit, caused the Bible to be written in man's language so that man could see the Word with his eyes and thereby put the Word in his heart.

By knowledge of God's spiritual laws, the man in Christ can once again exercise authority in the earth. You have the authority of Jesus to stop the effect of the curse in your life. He said: "Verily I say unto you, Whatsoever ye shall bind on earth shall be bound in heaven: and whatsoever ye shall loose on earth shall be loosed in heaven. Again I say unto you, That if two of you shall agree on earth as touching any thing that they shall ask, it shall be done for them of my Father which is in heaven" (Matthew 18:18-19).

Jesus the Healer

"Philip saith unto him, Lord, show us the Father, and it sufficeth us. Jesus saith unto him...he that hath seen me hath seen the Father... Believest thou not that I am in the Father, and the Father in me? the words that I speak unto you I speak not of myself: but the Father that dwelleth in me, he doeth the works" (John 14:8-10).

If you want to see the Father, look at Jesus. During His ministry on earth, Jesus revealed to men the express will of God in action. When you have seen Jesus, you have seen the Father.

Jesus did not even speak His own words, but the words He spoke were the Father's words. He did not take credit for the works done in His ministry, but said the Father in Him did the works.

Everything He said and did was a picture of the Father's will. Jesus said in John 8:28, "I do nothing of Myself (of My own accord, or on My own authority), but I say [exactly] what

My Father has taught Me" (*The Amplified Bible*). He was God's vehicle on the earth, God's way to man and man's way to God.

"For I came down from heaven, not to do mine own will, but the will of him that sent me" (John 6:38). "For this purpose the Son of God was manifested, that he might destroy the works of the devil" (1 John 3:8). Jesus came to do God's will in the earth. His will was for Jesus to destroy the works of the devil. God set Jesus in direct opposition to Satan, the curse and all its effects.

Every move that Jesus made and every word that He said was geared to destroy the work of Satan. Every work of power and every healing was the will of God.

> *Every move that Jesus made and every word that He said was geared to destroy the work of Satan.*

If you believe God's Word, you have to believe that Jesus' attitude toward sickness is God's attitude toward sickness.

"And great multitudes came unto him, having with them those that were lame, blind, dumb, maimed, and many others, and cast them down at Jesus' feet; and he healed them: Insomuch that the multitude wondered, when they saw the dumb to speak, the maimed to be whole, the lame to walk, and the blind to see: and they glorified the God of Israel" (Matthew 15:30-31).

"How God anointed Jesus of Nazareth with the Holy Ghost

and with power: who went about doing good, and healing all that were oppressed of the devil; for God was with him" (Acts 10:38).

"And ought not this woman, being a daughter of Abraham, whom Satan hath bound, lo, these eighteen years, be loosed from this bond on the sabbath day?" (Luke 13:16).

God's people were under the yoke of Satan. God sent Jesus to destroy Satan's work in their lives. Jesus operated as a prophet under the Abrahamic Covenant (Matthew 13:57). The people Jesus ministered to had a covenant of healing with God, but they did not walk in the light of that covenant. As heirs of Abraham, they should have been free.

Jesus could not be against sin without being against disease. His Father's Word opposed disease; therefore, Jesus opposed disease. Satan is the source of both. You cannot be against one and not the other.

Jesus preached deliverance to them and healed all that were oppressed by the devil. He taught them their covenant rights. He freed the people from evil spirits and healed their bodies of disease. He broke the yoke of Satan's oppression wherever He found it.

The woman who was bowed over and could not lift herself came to Him for help. Jesus laid His hands on her, and she was immediately made straight. His attitude was that this daughter of Abraham, whom Satan had bound for eighteen years, should be *loosed*. This was continually His response to the people who came to Him for help.

Sickness is a work of Satan. Jesus, fulfilling the will of God, stopped the effect of disease at every turn.

> *Sickness is a work of Satan. Jesus, fulfilling the will of God, stopped the effect of disease at every turn.*

"...A great multitude of people...came to hear him, and to be healed of their diseases; and they that were vexed with unclean spirits: and they were healed. And the whole multitude sought to touch him: for there went virtue out of him, and healed them all" (Luke 6:17-19). Jesus—the expression of God's will—*never* refused to heal *anyone*. Power (or virtue) was continually going forth from Him to heal *all*. Healing power was available to anyone who would receive it.

He never asked God if it was His will to heal an individual. He *knew* what God's attitude was toward sickness. He harbored no doubt about God's will in healing the multitudes.

The only record of anything hindering Jesus from accomplishing the will of God in the lives of His people occurred in Nazareth. Because it was His hometown, the people gave no honor to the ministry of Jesus. The Bible says, "And he did not many mighty works there because of their unbelief" (Matthew 13:58).

It was not *God's* will that stopped the work but *their* will—their *unbelief*. They were not willing to receive from the man they considered to be just the carpenter's son.

When Jesus sent His disciples out, He instructed them to "preach the kingdom of God, and to heal the sick" (Luke 9:2). He placed no limitation on the sick—*any* sick were to be healed if they would receive it. He told them to freely give what they had received.

The Scriptures have shown us beyond doubt that Jesus, fulfilling the will of God, offered healing **unconditionally** during His ministry on the earth.

Let's take one example from Acts to demonstrate the attitude of the early Church toward sickness. (Note: The early Church was not one church and the Church today another. The Body of Christ today, made up of all born-again people, is still the same church that came into existence on the day of Pentecost. What applied to the Church at Jerusalem still applies to the Church worldwide.) "There came also a multitude out of the cities round about unto Jerusalem, bringing sick folks, and them which were vexed with unclean spirits: and they were healed every one" (Acts 5:16).

Jesus told no one that he should keep his disease because God was trying to teach him something through sickness. No one in all the vast throngs and multitudes was told that God wanted him to stay sick in order to give Him glory. No, the scripture tells us that *healing* brings glory to God—not *sickness*. The people glorified the God of Israel "when they saw the dumb speak, the maimed be whole, the lame to walk, and the blind to see..." (Matthew 15:31).

Never did anyone come to Jesus for healing and receive, "It is not God's will to heal you," for an answer. "And, behold, there came a leper and worshipped him, saying, Lord, if thou wilt, thou canst make me clean. And Jesus put forth his hand, and touched him, saying, I will; be thou clean. And immediately his leprosy was cleansed" (Matthew 8:2, 3). Jesus straightened out the leper's theology in just two words, "I will." Healing is God's will or Jesus would not have healed *all* who came to Him.

We know with God there is no breach or deviation—no change. We know He is no respecter of persons (Acts 10:34). The ministry of Jesus is evidence of that.

The Bible teaches us a good tree can only bear good fruit. Jesus said that a good tree *cannot* bear evil fruit (Matthew 7:18).

God is good. He cannot be the source of any sickness. It is an abomination to His nature of love for people to believe God made them sick.

Some people say they know God does not make people sick, but they believe He allows Satan to put sickness on them to teach them or to get them into His will.

God does not have to allow Satan to do his evil work. Satan is quick to bring disease to Christians *if* they will allow it. It is *you* who must govern Satan in your life and circumstances.

If you are not walking in God's Word, you have no defense against Satan and his fruit of sickness. Your lack of knowledge of God's Word or your lack of diligence to act on that Word allows disease to fill your body.

God is *never* the source of sickness.

> *God is never the source of sickness.*

"Every good gift and every perfect gift is from above, and cometh down from the Father of lights, with whom is no variableness, neither shadow of turning" (James 1:17). *The Amplified Bible* says there can be no variation in Him. This is a key to knowing the source of everything that comes your way in life. According to scripture, we can say without reserve, "Every good gift is from above. Jesus came that we might have life."

Every evil, corrupt fruit is from Satan. Satan came to kill, to steal and to destroy. Anything that brings doubt, discouragement or defeat is from the enemy—*not from the Father.*

6 Faith in God's Mercy

Many Christians today have the same attitude as the leper in Mark 1:40-42. They believe that God *can* heal, but they doubt that He will heal *them.*

Many believe in His ability but not His mercy. They have no faith in God's love and mercy toward His family because they have no knowledge of His Word.

When speaking to the Syrophenician woman, Jesus called deliverance "the children's bread." If my children were hungry and knew I had bread but believed I would not give it to them, what an insult to my care, love and affection for them! I would prefer they believe I *could not* give them what they needed, than they believe I *would not.* I would much rather they doubt my ability than my love.

Theology teaches man about God's power, but for the most part denies His willingness to use that power on man's behalf.

Theology lacks the vital experience of the father-son relationship that we can enjoy in Jesus as children of God.

Man's idea of God always comes up short and lifeless. The mind of man is not capable of grasping that God is Love unless God's Spirit, through the Word, reveals it to him.

It is God's idea of God on which we must base our faith. It would be foolish to believe what man (who has never even seen Him) says about God, rather than to believe what He says about Himself.

"And the Lord descended in the cloud, and stood with him there, and proclaimed the name of the Lord. And the Lord passed by before him, and proclaimed, The Lord, The Lord God, merciful and gracious, longsuffering, and abundant in goodness and truth" (Exodus 34:5-6). God says of Himself that He is merciful and gracious, longsuffering (slow to anger) and abundant in goodness and truth.

The Bible magnifies God's mercy—His willingness to use His power to meet every need of man. The scripture speaks of the "exceeding greatness of his power to us-ward who believe..." (Ephesians 1:19). His power is directed *toward you* not *away from you.*

"The Lord is gracious, and full of compassion; slow to anger, and of great mercy" (Psalm 145:8). God is *full* of compassion and *great* mercy. Mercy and compassion are translated from the same Greek word.

Compassion is a moving or a yearning desire in the inward parts, the heart or spirit, toward another.[4] Compassion abides in the heart.

Jesus, in His high priestly ministry at the right hand of the Father, is moved by compassion or "touched" with our needs. "For we have not an high priest which cannot be touched with the feeling of our infirmities..." (Hebrews 4:15). He is moved by compassion toward us.

Time after time we see Jesus being moved by compassion and healing the sick during His earthly ministry. Compassion moved Him to extend God's hand of mercy to sufferers. It was the Father's compassion moving within Him. (Remember, He said He did nothing of Himself.) Because of His compassion, God's heart *yearns* to meet the needs of man.

> *Because of His compassion, God's heart yearns to meet the needs of man.*

One who does not know the Scriptures might wonder why, then, God does not heal all those who are sick regardless of their position of faith. God's mercy goes forth in accordance with His covenant, the Word. Because He has bound Himself by His Word, He can move freely only toward those who put themselves in a *position* to receive.

Acting on the Word puts you in this position to receive the mercy of God.

Mercy is God's attitude toward you in freely bestowing whatever is necessary to meet your needs. Mercy manifests itself in action and assumes the adequate resources to effect the proper result.[5]

Mercy is the result of compassion. The inward moving of compassion results in the outward manifestation necessary to meet the need.

> *Mercy is the result of compassion. The inward moving of compassion results in the outward manifestation necessary to meet the need.*

It is said of God in His Word that He *delighteth in mercy.* The Bible speaks of "the tender mercy of our God" and His "great mercy." With your spirit, dare to stretch your faith to take in the boundless mercy of God.

You are the object of God's mercy!

"O give thanks unto the Lord; for he is good: for his mercy endureth for ever" (Psalm 136:1).

"Know therefore that the Lord thy God, he is God, the faithful God, which keepeth covenant and mercy with them that love him and keep his commandments to a thousand generations" (Deuteronomy 7:9).

"For thou, Lord, art good, and ready to forgive; and plenteous in mercy unto all them that call upon thee" (Psalm 86:5).

His mercy endureth forever! His willingness to act on man's behalf is still operating in the earth. His mercy *never* runs out. Neither has it abated nor weakened.

His mercy continues toward those who love Him and do His Word. He is faithful to keep His covenant and offer His mercy.

It has been thousands of years since the Lord said His mercy extended to a thousand generations, and His mercy continues to reach you day after day. He is still plenteous in mercy toward them that call upon Him.

Praise the Lord! His mercy endureth forever! Mighty and powerful things happened when Israel said these words. They are words of praise and adoration to God.

When Solomon finished building the house of the Lord, the trumpeters and singers lifted their voices as one, and with trumpets, cymbals and instruments of music, they praised the Lord, saying, "For he is good: for his mercy endureth for ever."

The glory of God filled the house so that the priest could not even minister because of the cloud (2 Chronicles 5:13-14). God Himself inhabited the praises of His people.

Jehoshaphat appointed singers unto the Lord to go before the army and say, "Praise the Lord! For His mercy endureth forever."

When the Israelites began to sing and praise, the Lord set ambushes against their enemies and their enemies destroyed themselves (2 Chronicles 20:21-23).

The weapon of praise! Singers going before an army? It happened just that way. Israel never had to unsheathe a weapon of war—only to sing "Praise the Lord! For His mercy endureth forever!"

Speak of His Compassion and Mercy

We honor the Father when we believe His Word and magnify His love and mercy. We honor and praise Him when we speak of His goodness and lovingkindness. We honor Him when we speak of Him as our Father of love who does only good. So speak of the great God of the universe who is eager to bless and who even gave His own Son because He so loved the world! Speak of the Lord whose eyes "run to and fro throughout the whole earth to show Himself strong in behalf of those whose hearts are blameless toward Him..." (2 Chronicles 16:9, *The Amplified Bible*). When you speak of Him in this manner, you are praising Him. We are told to continually offer up to Him a sacrifice of praise (Hebrews 13:15).

David was a man after God's own heart. He knew how to praise His God. Until you have the Word dwelling in you richly so you can speak psalms and praises out of your own spirit, use the praises of David to magnify God. Speak them or sing them out loud to the Father.

"I will praise thee, O Lord, with my whole heart; I will show forth all thy marvellous works. I will be glad and rejoice in thee: I will sing praise to thy name, O thou most High. When mine enemies are turned back, they shall fall and perish at thy presence. For thou hast maintained my right and my cause; thou satest in the throne judging right" (Psalm 9:1-4).

The Word says God inhabits the praise of His people (Psalm 22:3). The enemy is turned back, falls and perishes at the presence of our God.

Praise not only honors God and empowers our faith, but it is also a powerful weapon where Satan is concerned. When we praise God, it works deliverance for us.

Abraham "...grew strong and was empowered by faith as he gave praise and glory to God" (Romans 4:20, *The Amplified Bible)*. As you praise God and speak of His marvelous

> *When we praise God, it works deliverance for us.*

works, your faith rises inside you to receive the blessings of God.

Honor God with the words of your mouth. Cause your words to agree with God's words where He is concerned. Look in His Word *for good things* to proclaim about Him. Proclaim the Lord's mercy and compassion to those around you. Tell others of the great things He has done in your life. Refuse to allow your words to be an affront to Father God and His nature of love.

Notice that David says, "I *will* praise...I *will* show forth thy marvellous works...I *will* be glad and rejoice...I *will* sing praise...." It is a matter of your will. You do not just praise God because you feel like it. You praise God because you *will* to praise Him.

Say with David, "I will praise thee, O Lord, with my

whole heart."

Great things happen when you continually confess the mercy of God. Faith rises up inside you. The reality that God loves you begins to sing through your spirit.

When God's mercy first became a reality to me, it was so alive in my heart that I continually confessed, "Praise the Lord. His mercy endureth forever." Something supernatural happened inside me; my faith rose to the knowledge of God's mercy and to the knowledge of that mercy continually surrounding me.

You are admonished to confess God's mercy in Psalm 118:4: "Let them now that fear the Lord say, that his mercy endureth for ever."

Now, put these words constantly on your lips. (For an example, look at Psalm 136.) You will begin to experience the thrill and joy of realizing God is indeed "rich in mercy" because of His great love for us (Ephesians 2:4).

As you confess God's mercy, you will expect and say, "Surely, goodness and mercy shall follow me all the days of my life."

You will realize mercy is continually coming out of the heart of God, still reaching through all generations to *you*.

"Let us therefore come boldly unto the throne of grace, that we may obtain mercy, and find grace to help in time of need" (Hebrews 4:16). Because of the Word, your faith has risen to the level of God's mercy. You are now in position to come boldly to the throne of grace and obtain mercy and find grace to help in time of need.

7
God's Medicine

"My son, attend to my words; incline thine ear unto my sayings. Let them not depart from thine eyes; keep them in the midst of thine heart. For they are life unto those that find them, and health to all their flesh. Keep thy heart with all diligence; for out of it are the issues of life" (Proverbs 4:20-23).

This is God's prescription for life and health!

"Attend to my words...." Give your undivided attention to God's Word and heed what He says. If you *attend* to someone you "take care of" that person. Give your time to the Word. Give thought and meditation to the Word. Give action to the Word. Continually give the Word first place in your life.

"Thou wilt keep him in perfect peace, whose mind is stayed on thee: because he trusteth in thee" (Isaiah 26:3). Your mind will be free from doubt when you keep your attention on God's Word. When you are trusting in God's Word you are trusting in Him. Stay your mind on the Word. Because you have committed yourself to God's Word, fear and doubt have been driven out. God's Word *will* keep you in perfect peace.

If you are not enjoying peace, you are not staying your mind on Him.

"Incline thine ear...." Open your understanding to take in God's sayings. Desire and pursue the knowledge of God's Word.

Put your physical ears in position to hear the Word of faith preached. Take your ears places where the Word is going forth. Faith comes by hearing the Word of God preached. Listen to what is being said with your spiritual ears. Jesus said,

> *God's Word will keep you in perfect peace.*

If any man has ears to hear, let him be listening, and let him perceive and comprehend. And He said to them, Be careful what you are hearing. The measure [of thought and study] you give [to the truth you hear] will be the measure [of virtue and knowledge] that comes back to you—and more [besides] will be given to you who hear. For to him who has will more be given; and from him who has nothing, even what he has will be taken away [by force] (Mark 4:23-25, *The Amplified Bible*).

Every man to whom Jesus was speaking had physical ears. Jesus was referring to receiving God's Word in the heart by listening to the Holy Spirit speak revelation knowledge.

Jesus is not talking about *passively* hearing. He said listen, perceive and comprehend, and even be careful *how* you hear.

The time you give to digesting the Word you hear will measure the return of virtue (power) and knowledge that will come back to you through the Word.

The man who hears (or receives revelation knowledge) will be given more. If you want to grow in the knowledge of God, be careful *how* you hear His Word.

"Let them not depart from thine eyes...." Keep your eyes trained on the Word of God. Do not look at circumstances or feelings that appear contrary to your healing. Look at God's Word. Give attention to what He says. Consider (or give thought to) God's Word instead of your body. Keep God's Word ever before your eyes. Jesus said, "The light of the body is the eye: if therefore thine eye be single, thy whole body shall be full of light" (Matthew 6:22).

This scripture reveals why it is so important that we not let the Word depart from our sight. The eye is the *gateway* to the body.

If your eye, or your attention, is on the darkness—the sickness—that is in your body, there will be no light to expel the darkness. The eye is unsound; therefore, the body is and will continue to be unsound. But cause your eye to be single on the Word of God and your *whole* body will be full of light. The single eye allows no darkness to enter.

What you do with your eyes in some cases is a matter of

life and death. To look at the sickness brings death. To look at God's Word brings life.

"Keep them in the midst of thine heart...." Allow God's Word to abide in you by meditating and acting on what you hear. The portion of God's Word that you act on is the portion of His Word that is abiding in you. Continually feed yourself with God's Word in order to keep the Word producing the force of faith.

Inclining your ear and refusing to allow the Word to depart from your eyes keeps God's Word alive in your heart.

> *God's words are life and health. The Word is God's medicine.*

"For they are life unto those that find them, and health to all their flesh...." God's Word is life. Jesus said, "My words are spirit and they are life." They are life to whom? They are life to those who find them and *health to all their flesh*. God's words are life and health. The Word is God's medicine.

Continually attending to the Word with your ears, your eyes and your heart will cause you to live in divine health. It will be as hard for you to get sick as it once was difficult for you to be healed because the power of the Word is continually being made life and health to your body.

By doing these things diligently, you are keeping your heart. "Keep thy heart with all diligence; for out of it are the issues of life" (Proverbs 4:23). From the midst of your heart are continually coming the forces (issues) of life, bringing

healing and health to your flesh. The Word in your heart produces life and health in your body.

Several times since I have learned to walk in faith, I have
failed to be diligent about keeping the Word before me, and
almost before I realized it, I became too sick to stay on my
feet. (I have learned since to go to the Word at the first sign
of a symptom—I immediately take a dose of God's medicine!)
I have turned to 1 Peter 2:24, read it aloud, and received my
healing. I have played the New Testament on tape and lis-
tened to the Word. I usually went to sleep listening. Either
the next morning or in a few hours, I awoke completely
healed. God's medicine has never failed to effect a healing
and a cure in my body. A few hours were as long as the
symptoms could stay.

This has only happened to me about three or four times
in many years. It would not have happened then if I had
not been busy with other things, instead of attending to
God's Word.

To be sick and receive healing was not God's best for me.
To receive healing is wonderful but to live in divine health is
better. We have learned to believe in divine health and not
just in healing. We maintain our health by the Word and do
not allow sickness to obtain a foothold.

To fill God's prescription for life and health, you must be
diligent in attending to His Word. You must give the Word
the place of authority and spend time in it *daily*. The forces

of life and power coming out of your heart will be in direct proportion to the amount of the Word going into you.

There is no limit to the amount of God's medicine you can take. You cannot get an overdose. The more you take, the more powerful you will become.

He Bore Our Sickness

"That it might be fulfilled which was spoken by Esaias the prophet, saying, Himself took our infirmities, and bare our sicknesses" (Matthew 8:17).

When Jesus bore away our sins, He also bore away our diseases. The Cross pronounced a double cure for the ills of mankind.

The Church of Jesus Christ has been made just as free from sickness as from sin. A Christian may continue to sin after he has been born again, but he *does not have to.* Sin can no longer enslave him unless he allows it (Romans 6:14).

A Christian may continue to be sick after he has been born again, but he *does not have to be.* He has been redeemed from sickness. The price has been paid for his healing. Sickness can no longer exert dominion over him unless he allows it.

Most believers have only known a part of their redemption. Their faith will operate to the degree of their knowledge of God's Word. They would have begun to live in divine health long ago had they realized that healing belonged to them.

As you accept the fact that as surely as Jesus bore your sins He also bore your disease, weakness and pain, your days of sickness will be over.

The light of the Word of God will destroy Satan's grip in your life in the area of physical suffering. The truth makes you free from his dominion when you realize that your healing has been purchased by the sacrifice of Jesus.

"Surely he hath borne our griefs, and carried our sorrows: yet we did esteem him stricken, smitten of God, and afflicted. But he was wounded for our transgressions, he was bruised for our iniquities: the chastisement of our peace was upon him; and with his stripes we are healed" (Isaiah 53:4-5).

The entire fifty-third chapter of Isaiah is about the substitution of Jesus for man. It says, "Surely he hath borne our griefs...." *Young's Analytical Concordance to the Bible* says *choli,* translated *griefs,* means "sickness, weakness and pain."

Surely He has borne your sickness, weakness and pain! Allow yourself to receive the magnitude of what God is speaking to you.

Jesus was smitten of God with sin and sickness in order for you to go free. Verse 6 tells us, "The Lord hath laid on him the iniquity of us all." Verse 10 says: "Yet it pleased the Lord to bruise him; he hath put him to grief...." (According to Dr. Young, the word *grief* means "to make sick" and should be translated, "He has made Him sick.")

According to the Word, what did Jesus do with your sickness? He bore it for you. It could not be God's will for you to be sick with the sickness that Jesus suffered for you.

Because God loved the world, He engineered the substitution of His only begotten Son to redeem man from the curse of Satan.

"Christ hath redeemed us from the curse of the law, being made a curse for us: for it is written, Cursed is every one that hangeth on a tree" (Galatians 3:13). Jesus was willing to take the curse in His own spirit, soul and body so that you would not have to continue under Satan's dominion.

There was no sickness before man became one with Satan. Sin is the root from which sickness came. Just as sin is the manifestation of spiritual death in the *heart* of man, sickness is the manifestation of spiritual death in the *body* of man.

Jesus came to destroy the works of the devil—*all* of his works (1 John 3:8). He did not destroy sin only to leave sickness in dominion. Partial redemption from Satan's power would not have pleased God, nor would it have fulfilled His plan for His family.

He redeemed the *whole* man—righteousness for his nature, peace for his mind and healing for his body. Redemption left nothing in

Jesus completely destroyed the works of the devil in the lives of men.

force that came upon man because of sin. Jesus completely
destroyed the works of the devil in the lives of men.

"For ye are bought with a price: therefore glorify
God in your body, and in your spirit, which are God's"
(1 Corinthians 6:20).

"And thus He fulfilled what was spoken by the prophet
Isaiah, He Himself took [in order to carry away] our weak-
nesses and infirmities and bore away our diseases" (Matthew
8:17, *The Amplified Bible*).

"Who his own self bare our sins in his own body on the
tree, that we, being dead to sins, should live unto righteousness: by whose stripes ye were healed" (1 Peter 2:24).

"By whose stripes ye *were* healed" is not a *promise*. It is a
fact. It has already taken place. Jesus bore your sickness and
by His stripes you *were* healed.

"For the Word that God speaks is alive and full of power
[making it active, operative, energizing, and effective]..."
(Hebrews 4:12, *The Amplified Bible*). The words spoken out
of the mouth of God are forever settled in heaven. When
He has said it once, He has said it forever. His words never
die nor lose their power.

"And God said, Let there be lights in the firmament
of the heaven to divide the day from the night..."
(Genesis 1:14). He does not have to get up every morning
about 4 o'clock and command the sun to rise and shine!
The Word He spoke at creation is still alive and full of

power, enforcing the result for which it was sent.

The words God spoke that day continue to operate the sun, moon and stars in their function of giving light to the earth. Because of His mighty words, "Let there be lights in the firmament," they would dare not cease to give forth their light.

His spoken Word has commanded lights to be in the firmament. His command is still in effect and will be until He changes it.

He has spoken His Word concerning your healing, too. This Word is also still in effect. Men *cannot* change it. Many have tried and have even said that healing has passed away. But *God* says that Jesus bore our sicknesses and carried our diseases, and by His stripes we were healed.

God's Word is alive!

God watches over His Word to perform it. His presence is ever over His Word to bring it to pass.

God's Word is to you now. This Word about healing has the power to accomplish the purpose for which it is sent—the healing of your body. It is just the same as if Jesus called you by name and said, "I bore your sicknesses and carried your diseases, and by My stripes you are healed."

When you have seen it in the Word, you have heard from God! Your healing would be no more valid and sure if Jesus appeared to you in person and spoke these words. Meditate and confess these scriptures about the substitution of Jesus for you until the reality of your healing literally dominates your mind and body.

9 Believe You Receive

Make the decision to live in divine health in the same way that you make the decision to accept Jesus as Savior. Decide to be well!

Just as salvation is being offered to whomever will accept it, so is healing being offered to whomever will believe.

The Greek word *sozo,* translated "saved" in Romans 10:9, is the same Greek word translated "healed" in the Gospels. In Mark 5:23, Jairus said to Jesus, "...I pray thee, come and lay thy hands on her, that she may be healed [sozo]; and she shall live." To the woman with the issue of blood, Jesus said, "Daughter, be of good comfort; thy faith hath made thee whole [sozo]" (Matthew 9:22).

When Jesus was raised from the dead, He purchased soundness for your spirit, soul and body. You have been made whole.

Right now, by faith, confess Jesus as your Healer in the same way that you made Him Lord over your life. Make Jesus

Lord over your body according to Romans 10:10: "According to the Word of God, I confess with my mouth that Jesus is Lord. I confess Him now as my Healer. I make Him Lord over my body. I believe in my heart that God raised Him from the dead. From this moment, my body is saved, healed, made whole and delivered."

Resist the temptation to be sick, just as you resist the temptation to sin. That may sound too simple, but it works because the Word says, "Resist the devil, and he will flee from you" (James 4:7).

Satan is the source of sickness. When he attempts to put sickness on your body, refuse it in the Name of Jesus. It is against the will of God for you to be sick. As soon as you have the slightest inclination that Satan is attempting to put sickness on you, turn to 1 Peter 2:24 and read it aloud. Receive it in faith and thank God that by His stripes you were healed.

You have an opportunity to "stand fast therefore in the liberty wherewith Christ hath made us free..." (Galatians 5:1). With His Name, His Word, His Spirit and Jesus as your Healer, you can enjoy divine health.

To get results, you must believe that you receive your healing *when you pray*—not after you are well. You are to join Abraham who "considered not his own body"...and consider instead what God says (Romans 4:19).

The symptoms of sickness may continue to linger after you believe that you receive. This is the time that you must hold fast to a fearless confession of the Word. "Do not, therefore, fling away your fearless confidence, for it carries a great and glorious compensation of reward. For you have need of steadfast patience and endurance, so that you may perform and fully accomplish the will of God, and thus receive and carry away [and enjoy to the full] what is promised" (Hebrews 10:35-36, *The Amplified Bible*).

Do not allow your fearless confidence in God's Word to be snatched away from you by Satan. This is walking by faith and not by sight.

E.W. Kenyon teaches that there are three witnesses in receiving healing: the Word, the pain or sickness and you. *You* are the deciding factor. If you join your confession with the pain, you are crossing the Word that says you are healed. If you align your confession with God's Word, you will have to cross the pain.

The Bible teaches that by two witnesses a thing is established. You make the choice. Agree with the pain and sickness will rule. But dare to agree with the Word and healing will be established. The circumstances will follow your action and confession.

Steadfastly and patiently know that God's Word *does not fail*. Refuse to be moved by what you see. The Word will change what you can see. Be moved by the Word and by your confession of Jesus as Healer.

Satan tried to tell you that you were not saved. He comes

to the new Christian with doubts of salvation. Now, his symptoms of pain or fever are trying to convince you that you are not healed. Stand fast in the knowledge of His Word.

Jesus told the nobleman, "Thy son liveth," and the Word says that the boy *began* to amend *from that hour* (John 4:51-53).

When you believe that you receive healing, you may be healed instantly or you may have to act on the covenant of healing, even though your body does not *feel* healed. One thing you know: When you believe that you receive, healing begins to take place in your body. God cannot keep His covenant without healing you—if you have met the conditions of that covenant.

You are learning to be moved by the Word, instead of by what you see or feel. This is how faith operates. You are becoming that faith man or woman you have yearned to be.

Your faith gets stronger as you use it to act on God's Word.

As you learn to stand against Satan and his symptoms, you will find it continues to become easier. But there is no formula that will work effectively unless you continually exert the force of faith through feeding on the Word.

Your faith gets stronger as you use it to act on God's Word.

If you will continually feed on God's Word, you will come to the place where you simply go to 1 Peter 2:24, enforce the Word that you *were* healed, thank God for His Word of healing and go on about your business.

Reference Sources

1. Vine, W.E., *An Expository Dictionary of New Testament Words,* (Old Tappan, N.J.: Flemming H. Revell Company, 1966), Vol. II p. 257.

2. Bosworth, F.F., *Christ the Healer,* p. 6.

3. Kenyon, E.W., *Jesus the Healer,* (Seattle, Wash.: Kenyon's Gospel Publishing Society, 1940), p. 61.

4. Vine, W.E., *An Expository Dictionary,* Vol. I, p. 218.

5. Vine, W.E., *An Expository Dictionary,* Vol. III, p. 60.

Prayer for Salvation and Baptism in the Holy Spirit

Heavenly Father, I come to You in the Name of Jesus. Your Word says, "Whosoever shall call on the name of the Lord shall be saved" (Acts 2:21). I am calling on You. I pray and ask Jesus to come into my heart and be Lord over my life according to Romans 10:9-10: "If thou shalt confess with thy mouth the Lord Jesus, and shalt believe in thine heart that God hath raised him from the dead, thou shalt be saved. For with the heart man believeth unto righteousness; and with the mouth confession is made unto salvation." I do that now. I confess that Jesus is Lord, and I believe in my heart that God raised Him from the dead. I repent of sin. I renounce it. I renounce the devil and everything he stands for. Jesus is my Lord.

I am now reborn! I am a Christian—a child of Almighty God! I am saved! You also said in Your Word, "If ye then, being evil, know how to give good gifts unto your children: HOW MUCH MORE shall your heavenly Father give the Holy Spirit to them that ask him?" (Luke 11:13). I'm also asking You to fill me with the Holy Spirit. Holy Spirit, rise up within me as I praise God. I fully expect to speak with other tongues as You give me the utterance (Acts 2:4). In Jesus' Name. Amen!

Begin to praise God for filling you with the Holy Spirit. Speak those words and syllables you receive—not in your own language, but the language given to you by the Holy Spirit. You have to use your own voice. God will not force you to speak. Don't be concerned with how it sounds. It is a heavenly language!

Continue with the blessing God has given you and pray in the spirit every day.

You are a born-again, Spirit-filled believer. You'll never be the same!

Find a good church that boldly preaches God's Word and obeys it. Become part of a church family who will love and care for you as you love and care for them.

We need to be connected to each other. It increases our strength in God. It's God's plan for us.

Make it a habit to watch the Believer's Voice of Victory Network and become a doer of the Word, who is blessed in his doing (James 1:22-25).

About the Author

Gloria Copeland is a noted author and minister of the gospel whose teaching ministry is known throughout the world. Believers worldwide know her through Believers' Conventions, Victory Campaigns, magazine articles, teaching audios and videos, and the daily and Sunday *Believer's Voice of Victory* television broadcast, which she hosts with her husband, Kenneth Copeland. She is known for Healing School, which she began teaching and hosting in 1979 at KCM meetings. Gloria delivers the Word of God and the keys to victorious Christian living to millions of people every year.

Gloria is author of the New York Times best-seller, *God's Master Plan for Your Life* and *Live Long, Finish Strong*, as well as numerous other favorites, including *God's Will for You, Walk With God, God's Will Is Prosperity, Hidden Treasures* and *To Know Him*. She has also co-authored several books with her husband, including *Family Promises, Healing Promises* and the best-selling daily devotionals, *From Faith to Faith* and *Pursuit of His Presence*.

She holds an honorary doctorate from Oral Roberts University. In 1994, Gloria was voted Christian Woman of the Year, an honor conferred on women whose example demonstrates outstanding Christian leadership. Gloria is also the co-founder and vice president of Kenneth Copeland Ministries in Fort Worth, Texas.

Materials to Help You Receive Your Healing by Gloria Copeland

Books

* And Jesus Healed Them All
* God's Prescription for Divine Health
* God's Will for Your Healing
* Harvest of Health

Words That Heal (gift book with CD enclosed)

Audio Resources

Be Made Whole—Live Long, Live Healthy

God Is a Good God

God Wants You Well

Healing Confessions (CD and minibook)

Healing School

DVD Resources

Be Made Whole—Live Long, Live Healthy

Know Him As Healer

*Available in Spanish

When The LORD first spoke to Kenneth and Gloria Copeland about starting the *Believer's Voice of Victory* magazine...

He said: *This is your seed. Give it to everyone who ever responds to your ministry, and don't ever allow anyone to pay for a subscription!*

For more than 50 years, it has been the joy of Kenneth Copeland Ministries to bring the good news to believers. Readers enjoy teaching from ministers who write from lives of living contact with God, and testimonies from believers experiencing victory through God's WORD in their everyday lives.

Today, the *BVOV* magazine is mailed monthly, bringing encouragement and blessing to believers around the world. Many even use it as a ministry tool, passing it on to others who desire to know Jesus and grow in their faith!

Request your FREE subscription to the *Believer's Voice of Victory* magazine today!

Go to **freevictory.com** to subscribe online, or call us at **1-800-600-7395** (U.S. only) or **+1-817-852-6000**.

We're Here for You!®

Your growth in God's WORD and victory in Jesus are at the very center of our hearts. In every way God has equipped us, we will help you deal with the issues facing you, so you can be the **victorious overcomer** He has planned for you to be.

The mission of Kenneth Copeland Ministries is about all of us growing and going together. Our prayer is that you will take full advantage of all The LORD has given us to share with you.

Wherever you are in the world, you can watch the *Believer's Voice of Victory* broadcast on television (check your local listings), the Internet at kcm.org or on our digital Roku channel.

Our website, **kcm.org,** gives you access to every resource we've developed for your victory. And, you can find contact information for our international offices in Africa, Australia, Canada, Europe, Ukraine and our headquarters in the United States.

Each office is staffed with devoted men and women, ready to serve and pray with you. You can contact the worldwide office nearest you for assistance, and you can call us for prayer at our U.S. number, +1-817-852-6000, 24 hours every day!

We encourage you to connect with us often and let us be part of your everyday walk of faith!

Jesus Is LORD!

Kenneth & Gloria Copeland

Kenneth and Gloria Copeland